HA!

HA!

KT-458-046

LAUGH

ON

THE

LOO

HAHA!

NUMBER TWO!

This edition published in 2020 by Ginger Fox®
an imprint of Hacche Retail Ltd
Stirling House, College Road, Cheltenham GL53 7HY
United Kingdom

Compiled by Leigh Cooke in collaboration with Hacche Retail Ltd

First published in 2020 by Ginger Fox®

www.gingerfox.co.uk
Follow us!
Facebook: GingerFoxUK
Instagram: GingerFoxUK
Twitter: GingerFox_UK

ISBN: 978-1-911006-73-2

10 9 8 7 6 5 4 3 2 1

Printed and bound in China

CONTENTS

WHAT'S THE DIFFERENCE BETWEEN

ENGLAND

and a

TEABAG

and other quintessentially
BRITISH BUFFOONERY

"We should go for a drink sometime."
TRANSLATION:
I never want to see you again.

"Yeah, could do."
TRANSLATION:
Absolutely not.

"It's not quite what I had in mind."
TRANSLATION:
I hate it.

"A bit of a pickle."
TRANSLATION:
A catastrophe of epic proportions.

"That's one way of looking at it."
TRANSLATION:
You're wrong.

"With the greatest respect..."
TRANSLATION:
I think you're an idiot.

"You look as though you had
a good time last night."
TRANSLATION:
You look awful.

"Could we consider some
other options?"
TRANSLATION:
I don't like your idea.

"Not for me, thank you."
TRANSLATION:
Please ask again so I can say, "Oh, go on then."

TWO-WORD PHRASES GUARANTEED TO SEND SHIVERS DOWN YOUR SPINE:

"They're here."   "Help yourself."

"Battery died."   "Pop round."

"Let's dance."   "No milk."

I'm sure, wherever Dad is, he's looking down on us.

He's still alive... just very condescending.

What time does Andy Murray go to bed? Tennish.

There are only two occasions upon which it is acceptable to wake someone up before 6am.

Snow. Or the death of a celebrity.

You know you're British when summer is your favourite day of the year.

YOU'RE PAINFULLY BRITISH IF:

You introduce yourself by beginning with, "I'm sorry."

You end an email with "Thanks", as a warning that you are perilously close to losing your cool.

You didn't quite catch someone's name, so avoid ever talking to them again.

You receive a text saying, "Still want to meet later?" and feel instantly gutted.

You see that somebody is about to ring your doorbell, so potter around looking busy until it happens.

You touch your bag or do up your coat five minutes before your stop on the bus to give the person next to you the heads-up.

You concentrate so hard on eye contact that you have no idea what's being said.

You find yourself unable to stand and leave anywhere without saying, "Right..."

There's someone at the supermarket browsing the item you want, so you pretend to look at things you don't want until they move on.

You don't know what to do with your face when you open a present.

You use 😂 in a text when all you've done is breathe through your nostrils harder.

Why is England such a wet country?

Because the Queen has reigned there for years.

WHAT'S THE DIFFERENCE BETWEEN ENGLAND AND A TEABAG? THE TEABAG STAYS IN THE CUP LONGER.

What is the longest word in the English language?

Smiles. (There's a mile between its first and last letters.)

What do you do if you're driving your car in central London and you see a space man?

Park in it, man.

Only in Britain... do we leave cars worth thousands of pounds on the drive and put our junk in the garage.

How long does it take to ship tea from China to England?

Oolong time.

———

Why do hipsters only drink iced tea?

Because ice was water before it was cool.

———

Bacon and eggs walk into a bar one morning.

The bartender glances up and says, "Sorry, we don't serve breakfast."

Did you hear about the man who drowned in his breakfast cereal?

He was dragged under by a strong currant.

What is the height of optimism?

An English batsman putting on sunscreen.

Being British is about driving a
GERMAN car to an **IRISH** pub for a
BELGIAN beer, then travelling home —
grabbing an **INDIAN** curry or a
TURKISH kebab on the way — to sit
on **SWEDISH** furniture watching
AMERICAN shows on a **JAPANESE** TV.

BRITAIN'S FUNNIEST PLACE NAMES:

BROKENWIND   A hamlet in Aberdeenshire, Scotland

LOOSE BOTTOM   A scenic area popular with walkers, close to Falmer in East Sussex, England

GREAT SNORING   A sleepy rural village in Norfolk, England

BARTON IN THE BEANS   A hamlet in Leicestershire, England – once renowned for cultivating broad beans

DULL   A village in Perthshire, Scotland, twinned with Boring in Oregon, USA, and Bland in New South Wales, Australia

HORRID HILL   Part of the Riverside Country Park in Kent, England

DROOP   A hamlet in Dorset, England

CRACKPOT   A village in North Yorkshire, England

BOTUS FLEMING   A village in Cornwall, England

STRANAGALWILLY   A townland in County Tyrone, Northern Ireland

SCRATCHY BOTTOM   A clifftop valley between Durdle Door and Swyre Head in Dorset, England

What did the
GRAPE
say when it was

AND OTHER
BOOZY BANTER

Warning: Excessive alcohol consumption can cause memory loss.

Or, worse still, memory loss.

———

Doctor: Do you drink to excess?

Patient: Yep, I'll drink to anything.

———

I gave up alcohol last year.
Worst 15 minutes of my life.

———

Proudly showing off his new flat to friends late one night, a slightly tipsy
man led the way through to his bedroom, where there was a big brass gong.
"What's that for?" one of the guests asked.
"That's the talking clock," the man replied.
"How does it work?" asked his friend.
"Watch!" the man said, giving it a whack with a hammer.
Suddenly, someone on the other side of the wall screamed, "For goodness'
sake, it's two o'clock in the morning!"

PATIENT: Doctor, do you think that I will live until I'm 100?

DOCTOR: How old are you now?

PATIENT: Forty.

DOCTOR: Do you drink alcohol, smoke or have any other vices?

PATIENT: No.

DOCTOR: Then what's the point?

A man walks into a bar and says, "A Scotch, please."
The bartender hands him the drink and says, "That'll be five pounds."
The man replies, "What are you talking about? I don't owe you anything for this."
A lawyer, sitting nearby and overhearing the conversation, tells the bartender,
"He's got you there. In the original offer, which constitutes a binding contract
upon acceptance, there was no stipulation of remuneration."
The bartender is not impressed, but lets the man have the drink anyway.
The next day, the same man walks into the bar.
The bartender says, "I can't believe you've got the nerve to come back!"
The man says, "What are you talking about? I've never been in this place in my life."
The bartender replies, "I'm sorry. You must have a double."
To which the man replies, "Thank you. Make it a Scotch."

This wine tastes a lot like I'm not going to work tomorrow.

A man walks into a bar carrying a pair of jump leads.
The lady behind the bar eyes him and says,
"Now, don't start anything..."

I WOKE UP TO THE SOUND OF MY NEIGHBOUR MOWING THE LAWN.

HE'LL JUST HAVE TO GO AROUND ME.

I ran out of coffee this morning.
Wine seemed like a good alternative.

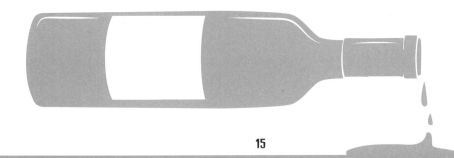

A drunk man staggers into a church and silently sits down in the confession box. The confused priest coughs to get his attention, but the man says nothing.

The priest then knocks on the wall three times in an attempt to get the man to speak.

Finally, the man replies, "Sorry, mate. There's no paper in this one either."

What did the grape say when it was crushed?

Nothing, it just let out a little wine.

"Can I have a wine, please?"
"This is McDonald's."
"Oh, sorry, can I have a McWine, please?"

A man is in bed with his wife when there is a bang on the door.
"I'm not getting out of bed at this time," he says, and rolls over.
Then, a louder knock follows.
"Aren't you going to answer that?" asks his wife. So he goes downstairs,
opens the front door and sees a drunk man standing there.
"Hello," slurs the stranger. "Can you give me a push?"
"No, it's half past three. I was in bed," the man replies and slams the door.
He goes back up to bed and tells his wife what happened and she says,
"That wasn't very nice of you. Remember that night we broke down in
the pouring rain on the way to pick the children up from the babysitter
and you had to knock on that man's door to get us started again?
What would have happened if he'd told us to get lost?"
"But this man was drunk," the husband answers.
"It doesn't matter," says the wife. "He needs our help. Go and help him."
So the husband gets out of bed again and goes downstairs. He opens the
door and, not being able to see the stranger anywhere, shouts,
"Hey, do you still want a push? Where are you?"
The drunk man replies, "I'm over here, on the swing!"

A dog walks into a bar and asks the bartender, "Do you have any jobs?"
The bartender replies, "No, why don't you try the circus?"
The dog looks confused and responds, "Why would the circus need bar staff?"

I enjoy a glass of wine each evening for its health benefits.
The other glasses are for my witty comebacks and my flawless dance moves.

When you get a hangover from wine, it's called The Grape Depression.

It doesn't matter if the glass is half empty or half full.

There's clearly room for more wine.

I've trained my dog to bring me a glass of red wine.

It's a Bordeaux collie.

I'm a wine enthusiast.

The more wine I drink, the more enthusiastic I get.

Wine improves with age. I improve with wine.

Every raisin is a tragic tale of a grape that could have been wine.

Doctors and vintners have got together and invented a new grape variety
that acts as an anti-diuretic, to help with incontinence.

It's called Pinot More.

The past, the present and the future walk into a bar.

It was tense.

Two chemists walk into a bar. The first chemist says,
"I'll have a glass of H_2O."
The second chemist says, "I'll have a glass of H_2O too."
The second chemist dies.

A grasshopper walks into a bar and the bartender says,
"Hey, we have a drink named after you!"
The grasshopper looks surprised and says,
"You have a drink called Gary?"

CHARLES DICKENS WALKS INTO A BAR AND ORDERS A MARTINI.

THE BARTENDER ASKS, "OLIVE OR TWIST?"

A snake slithers into a bar and asks for a pint.
The bartender replies, "Sorry, but I can't serve you."
"Why not?" asks the snake.
"You can't hold your beer."

The bartender says, "We don't serve time travellers in here."
A time traveller walks into a bar.

WHY IS LIFE

LIKE A
ROLL OF

TOILET
PAPER

AND OTHER GAGS FOR THE GOLDEN YEARS

Father: Thank goodness you're home, son. I've been trying to call you for hours.
Son: Dad, that's a calculator.

———

When your elderly relatives come up to you at weddings and say,
"You're next", try doing the same to them at funerals.

———

An elderly man was driving with a friend when he went straight
through a red light. His friend was shocked, but politely said nothing.
Then the man drove through another red light.
The friend said, "Do you realise you just drove through two red lights?"
"Uhhhh," said the man, "I thought you were driving!"

———

Life is like a roll of toilet paper:
the closer you get to the end, the faster it goes.

MIDDLE AGE IS...

...when you go to bed still thinking you'll feel better in the morning.

...when you finally get your head together, and then your body starts falling apart.

OLD AGE IS...

...realising you have a suppository in your ear and wondering where on earth your hearing aid is.

...when your friends compliment you on your stylish faux-alligator shoes, and you're actually barefoot.

...when an 'all-nighter' means not getting up to use the bathroom.

...when people wake you up from a nice nap to make sure you're still alive.

...all about multitasking – being able to laugh, cough, sneeze and pee all at the same time.

...when the candles cost more than the cake.

Three elderly sisters shared a house together.
One evening, the 96-year-old went upstairs to have a bath.
As she was stepping into it, she paused. Then she called out to her two sisters,
"Was I getting into the bath or getting out of it?"
"You old fool," said the 94-year-old. "I'll come up and see."
When she got halfway up the stairs, she paused. Then she called downstairs
to her other sister, "Was I going up the stairs or coming down them?"
Her 92-year-old sister was sitting at the kitchen table drinking a cup of tea,
and thought to herself, "I'll never get that forgetful, knock on wood."
She knocked twice on the table, shook her head and called out,
"I'll be up to help you both as soon as I've seen who's at the door."

PARTY GAMES FOR YOUR SECOND CHILDHOOD:

Sag, you're it

Kick the bucket

Simon says something incoherent

Hide and pee

Musical recliners

He's so old that, when he orders a hard-boiled egg in a café,
they ask for the money upfront.

THE PERKS OF GETTING OLD:

Anything that you buy now won't wear out.

Your secrets are safe with your friends

(because they can't remember them).

Kidnappers are not very interested in you.

In a hostage situation, you're likely to be released first.

There is nothing left to learn the hard way.

Your supply of brain cells is finally down to a manageable size.

Your investment in health insurance is finally paying off.

Your joints are more accurate meteorologists than the BBC.

Nobody calls you after 9pm in case they wake you.

You've (probably) finished paying back your student loan.

A widowed man is on holiday and he heads for the beach, hoping to make some female friends. Much to his surprise, all the ladies at the beach bar seem to be admiring a really old man strolling along the shore.

Later that evening, he sees the same old man surrounded by beautiful women. The widower takes him to one side and asks, "What's your secret?" The old man replies, "Try putting a potato down your trunks."

The thankful widower can't wait for the following day to try his luck again. The next morning he goes out to the beach, with a large potato tucked neatly into his trunks. The ladies on the beach smile at him, but move on.

That evening, the widower finds the old man again and asks for more help. The old man responds, "Yes, I saw you at the beach today. Next time, try putting the potato down the front of your trunks."

Daughter: Daddy, what's a hipster?

Father: Someone who wears something just to look different. They often buy their clothes in charity shops, wear thick glasses and grow a beard.

Daughter: Is Grandma a hipster?

Why do grandparents smile all the time?

Because they can't hear what anyone's saying.

My nine-year-old daughter walked in while I was getting ready for work.

"What are you doing?" she asked.

"Putting on my wrinkle cream," I answered.

"Oh," she said, walking away, "I thought they were natural."

TEXTING SHORTHAND FOR THE NOT-SO-YOUNG:

ATD:	At The Doctor's
BFF:	Best Friend's Funeral
BTW:	Bring The Wheelchair
BYOT:	Bring Your Own Teeth
CGU:	Can't Get Up
DWI:	Driving While Incontinent
FWB:	Friend With Beta-blockers
FWIW:	Forgot Where I Was
FYI:	Found Your Insulin
GGPBL:	Gotta Go, Pacemaker Battery Low
GHA:	Got Heartburn Again
HGBM:	Had Good Bowel Movement
IMHO:	Is My Hearing-aid On?
LMDO:	Laughing My Dentures Out
OMMR:	On My Massage Recliner
ROFL... CGU:	Rolling On Floor Laughing... Can't Get Up
WAITT:	Who Am I Talking To?
GGLKI:	Gotta Go, Laxative Kicking In

WHERE DID THE

SHEEP

go on

HONEYMOON

JUST MARRIED

and other
HOLIDAY HILARITY

FIRST MAN: My son came to visit for the summer holidays.

SECOND MAN: That's nice. Did you meet him at the airport?

FIRST MAN: No, I've known him for years.

———

A young man checks into a hotel for the first time in his life and goes up to his room. Five minutes later, he calls reception and says, "You've given me a room with no exit. How do I get out?!" The receptionist says, "Sir, that's absurd. Have you looked for the door?" The young man says, "Well, there's one door that leads to the bathroom. There's a second door that goes into the wardrobe. And there's a last door I haven't tried, but it has a 'Do not disturb' sign on it."

What's the worst thing you can hear when you're wearing a bikini? "Good for you!"

Where did the sheep go on honeymoon?

The Baa-hamas.

A farmer went on his first city break to see the sights of London. After booking into his hotel, he asked the receptionist what time meals were served in the restaurant.
The receptionist explained, "Breakfast is served from 7 to 11, lunch from 12 to 3 and dinner is from 6 to 8."
"But when am I going to get time to see the city?" asked the baffled farmer.

I find it so exciting trying to pack myself into a small suitcase.
I can hardly contain myself.

What do you call a snowman on a beach holiday?
A puddle.

I'm not saying our hotel was cheap,
but the Bible only had seven commandments.

What do you call six weeks of rain in the UK?

Summer.

A passenger was travelling on holiday on a budget airline.

"Would you like dinner?" the cabin crew asked.

"What are my choices?"

"Yes or no."

A man arrived at a seaside hotel, where he had made a reservation late
that evening. All the lights were out, so he knocked on the door.
After a long time, a light appeared at an upstairs window and a woman
called out, "Who are you? What do you want?"
"I'm staying here," shouted the man.
"OK," she replied, and slammed the window shut.

A father decides to take his son camping for the first time. After they have set up camp in the woods, the boy asks his dad where he can go to the toilet. "That's the beauty of camping in the woods," the father replies, "you can go to the toilet wherever you want."

A few minutes later, the young lad wanders back up to his dad.

"So, where did you go to the toilet then, Son?" his father asks.

"In your tent," the boy replies.

The closest I get to camping is staying in a hotel with no Wi-Fi.

I slept like a log last night.
I woke up on the campfire.

Going camping is the perfect reminder of how great life is when you're not camping.

———

If you're sleeping in something that has wheels, you're not camping, you're parking.

A man went into a camping shop and said, "I would like to buy a tent." The man behind the counter said, "To camp?" The customer said (in a much gruffer, more manly tone), "Sorry, I would like to buy a tent."

Sherlock Holmes and Dr Watson go camping and pitch their tent in a clearing in the woods. During the night, Holmes wakes his companion and says, "Watson, look up at the stars and tell me what you deduce." Watson looks pensive for a moment and then replies, "I see millions of stars, and if even a few of those have planets it's quite likely there are some planets like Earth, and if there are a few planets like Earth out there, there might also be life..."

Holmes replies, "Watson, you idiot. Somebody stole our tent."

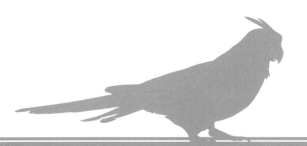

A magician was working on a cruise ship in the Caribbean.
The audience was new each week, so he always did the same tricks.
The problem was, the captain's pet parrot saw all the shows and
began to understand how the magician did every trick.
It started squawking in the middle of the show, "Look, it's not the same hat!
Look, he's hiding the flowers under the table! Hey, why are all the cards
the ace of spades?"
The magician was furious but, as it was the captain's parrot, there wasn't
much he could do about it. Then, one day, the cruise ship ran aground and sank.
The magician found himself cast adrift on a piece of wood with the parrot.
They glared at each other but said nothing. Finally, after a week,
the parrot said, "OK, I give up. Where's the boat?"

What do you call a Frenchman wearing sandals?

Phillipe Phloppe.

I'm not saying our holiday was dull,
but even the tide went out and didn't come back.

A cruise ship was circling a desert island. Everyone on board could see a bearded man on the island, shouting and desperately waving his hands.
"Who is it?" a passenger asked the captain.
The captain replied, "I've no idea, but every year when we pass he goes bananas."

Where do sharks go on summer holiday? Finland!

Two friends are talking over lunch one day. The first friend says,
"Sally, remind me, where did your sister go on holiday?"
"Alaska," her friend replies.
"Never mind, I'll ask her myself," says the first friend.

One dog asked another, "Where do fleas go on holiday?"

The second dog replied, "Search me!"

WHAT MAKE OF

COMPUTER

has the best

SINGING

VOICE

and other
MODERN-LIFE MADNESS

Social media: a way to reconnect with the people you couldn't be bothered to keep in touch with.

———

They call it a selfie because 'narcissistie' is too hard to spell.

———

THANK GOODNESS FOR FACEBOOK OR I'D HAVE TO CALL 598 PEOPLE AND TELL THEM HOW FAR I RAN TODAY.

———

Me: Don't you worry that Facebook is killing meaningful communication?
Friend: Like.

———

The worst thing about Twitter being down is not being able to tweet jokes about Twitter being down.

———

I put my Grandma on speed dial.
I call that Instagran.

———

Mark Zuckerberg bought Instagram for $1,000,000,000???
He could have downloaded it for free.

———

I wonder what Facebook employees do to waste time at work?

YOU KNOW YOU'RE ADDICTED TO FACEBOOK IF:

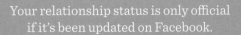

You read lists that claim to tell you whether you're addicted to Facebook.

Your relationship status is only official if it's been updated on Facebook.

You have Facebook 'friends' who you've never actually met in real life.

Before you accept a job offer, you check out the company's Facebook-use policies.

You no longer buy a newspaper, as you get all your current affairs from your 'news' feed.

You share things on Facebook that you'd never tell anyone in real life.

Even your pet has a Facebook profile.

Your mood can be affected for days if something you post doesn't get any likes.

You've already checked your Facebook account three times while reading this list.

A man tells his doctor,
"Doctor, help me. I'm addicted to Twitter!"
The doctor replies, "Sorry, I don't follow you."

———

What is Forrest Gump's computer password?

1Forrest1

———

What make of computer has the best singing voice?
A Dell.

———

I decided to make my password 'incorrect' because if
I mistype or forget it, my computer will remind me,
"Your password is incorrect."

———

How easy is it to count in binary?

It's as easy as 01 10 11.

YOU REALLY LIVE IN THE MODERN WORLD IF YOU...

...swoop in and stop the microwave with one second left
so you don't hear the beep.

...feel like a Jedi Knight when you stand in front of an
automatic sliding door.

...don't start eating a TV dinner until you find the
perfect show to watch.

...say "I have plans" to get out of other plans, when the only
thing you have planned is Netflix.

...ignore an awkward text for days then reply,
"OMG! I'm SO sorry, just noticed my reply didn't go through!"

...are unable to go for a #2 without your smartphone.

...put your music on shuffle, only to skip all the songs
until you find the one you want.

...pull out your phone to check the time, only to realise you
have to do it again because you forgot to look at the clock.

...throw away the box from your microwave meal,
then immediately have to fish it back out of the bin
to find out how long to cook the food for.

TRANSLATING WORK EMAILS

I have a question = I have 18 questions.

I'll look into it = I've already forgotten about it.

I'll do my best = I'll do the bare minimum.

I'm happy to discuss further = Don't ask me about this ever again.

No worries = You really messed up this time.

Take care = This is the last you'll ever hear from me.

Cheers = I have no respect for you or myself.

I look forward to hearing your thoughts =
Reply to me immediately, or else.

I know you're busy = You never respond to me and
you're not that important.

Sent from my iPhone, sorry for the typos =
I'm too lazy to check my spelling.

FIRST WORLD PROBLEMS:

I ate too much food for lunch and now I'm tired.

I only just upgraded my phone, and now they've released a new one.

I spread cold butter on my bread and it ripped.

'United Kingdom' wasn't at the top of the drop-down menu.

I'm too hot with a jumper on, but too cold without it.

My commute to work is too short – the inside of my car doesn't have time to warm up before I get there and I never have time to listen to a whole song.

One click on my mechanical pencil isn't enough, but two clicks are too much.

I hoovered up a spider and now I'm afraid to switch the Hoover off.

I accidentally bought conditioner when I needed to buy shampoo.

My shampoo and conditioner never run out at the same time.

Some caveman paid me by cheque, so now I have to go to the bank to pay it in.

My towel is still wet from the first shower I had today.

The pizza-delivery person can't find my house so now I have to stand outside and wave like an idiot.

My bottled water is too cold and it's hurting my teeth.

My smartphone changes 'lol' to 'LOL', making me sound more amused than I actually am.

I want to get an inspirational tattoo, but my life has been too easy.

My car lost its new-car smell.

I want to lie on my side to look at my smartphone, but the screen keeps rotating.

I want to eat crisps and watch TV, but I can't hear the TV above my crunching.

It's boiling hot outside, but freezing in my air-conditioned office.

My biscuit is too big to dunk in my cup of tea.

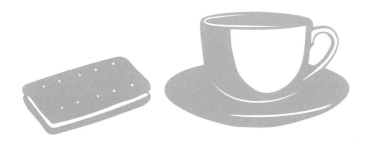

WHY DID THE MP

CROSS

THE ROAD

and other

POLITICAL
PECULIARITIES

Politicians and nappies have one thing in common:
they should both be changed regularly. For the same reason.

———

What's the difference between a politician and a snail?

One is a slimy pest that leaves a trail everywhere,
and the other is a snail.

———

THE PRIME MINISTER HAS ANNOUNCED
THAT NO MPS WILL BE ABLE TO CLAIM
FURNITURE EXPENSES FROM NOW ON.
IT WAS A CABINET DECISION.

———

A little girl asks her dad, "Do all fairy tales begin with 'Once upon a time...'?"
Her dad replies, "No, some begin with 'If I am elected...'"

———

What's the difference between parliament and a catering service?
One books the cooks...

An MP, a clergyman and a girl scout were passengers on a small plane that developed engine trouble. The pilot announced, "We'll have to jump out." Unfortunately, there were only three parachutes.

The pilot said, "I have a wife and seven small children. My family needs me. I'm taking one of the parachutes and jumping out!" And he jumped.

Then the MP said, "I am the smartest politician in the world. The country needs me. I'm taking one of the parachutes." And she jumped.

The clergyman said to the scout, "I've had a good life and yours is still ahead of you. You take the last parachute."

The girl shrugged and said, "It's OK. There are two parachutes left. The smartest politician in the world just jumped out of the plane wearing my backpack!"

What's the difference between a duck and George Washington?

One has a bill on his face and the other has his face on a bill.

I don't approve of political jokes,
I've seen too many get elected.

An MP sits in his office. Out of boredom, he decides to see what's inside his old filing cabinet. He looks through the contents and comes across an antique brass lamp.

"This will look good in my study," he thinks, and takes it home with him. Later, while polishing the lamp, a genie appears and grants him three wishes. "I would like an ice-cold beer," says the MP. He gets his beer and drinks it. He then states his second wish. "I wish to be on an island surrounded by beautiful women who find me irresistible."

Suddenly, the MP finds himself on an island surrounded by women, all eyeing him lustfully. He tells the genie his third and last wish. "I wish I never have to work again."

Instantly he finds himself back in his government office.

A politician is someone who shakes your hand before an election – and your confidence after it.

The government claims it is following the will of the people.

I didn't even know we'd died.

ELECTILE DYSFUNCTION:
The inability to become aroused over any of the choices on your ballot paper.

Democracy is the counting of heads, regardless of the contents.

Democracy is being allowed to vote for the candidate you dislike least.

The best argument against democracy is a five-minute conversation with the average voter.

Democracy is three wolves and one sheep voting on what to have for supper.

Politics is supposed to be the second oldest profession. I have come to realise that it bears a very close resemblance to the first.

PECULIAR (BUT REAL) POLITICAL PARTIES:

Sun Ripened Warm Tomato Party (Australia)

Beer Lovers Party (Belarus)

Canadian Extreme Wrestling Party (Canada)

Rhinoceros Party (Canada)

Friends of Beer Party (Czech Republic)

Union of Conscientiously Work-Shy Elements (Denmark)

Hungarian Two-Tailed Dog Party (Hungary)

Beer Unity Party (Norway)

Polish Beer-Lovers' Party (Poland)

Beer Lovers Party (Russia)

Donald Duck Party (Sweden)

Ukrainian Beer Lovers Party (Ukraine) ...*do you notice a theme here?*

Official Monster Raving Loony Party (UK)

Teddy Bear Alliance (UK)

Surprise Party (USA)

NON-HUMAN ELECTORAL CANDIDATES:

A brown mule called Boston Curtis (USA)

A rhinoceros called Cacareco (Brazil)

A boar hog called Pigasus the Immortal (USA)

A gorilla called Colossus (USA)

A cat called Morris (Mexico)

A puppet called Dustin the Turkey (Republic of Ireland)

A dachshund called Saucisse (France)

A sock puppet called Ed the Sock (Canada)

A crawfish called Crawfish B (USA)

A cocker spaniel called Comandante Chispas (Ecuador)

Why did the MP cross the road?

So he could claim a second-home allowance.

———

Politics is the art of looking for trouble, finding it, misdiagnosing it
and then misapplying the wrong remedies.

TO ERR IS HUMAN.
TO BLAME SOMEONE ELSE IS POLITICS.

Why don't you ever hear about burglars robbing politicians?

Professional courtesy.

———

What does a politician use for birth control?

Their personality.

———

Political party broadcasts prove one thing:
a party can cover all its best points in less than a minute.

———

If con is the opposite of pro, then what is the opposite of progress?

———

I have realised why politicians do nothing to improve
the quality of state-school education.
They are terrified of educated voters.

HOW MANY

TEENAGERS

DOES IT TAKE
TO CHANGE A

LIGHT BULB

and other
CHILDHOOD CHUCKLES

I don't ever need to use Google –
my child knows everything.

DAD: ARE YOU FIRST IN ANYTHING AT SCHOOL?
SON: I'M FIRST OUT WHEN THE BELL RINGS.

Teacher: In this box, I have a ten-foot snake.
Pupil: You can't fool me. Snakes don't have feet.

Billy's teacher always rewarded good work by putting
a gold star at the top of his homework.
One day Billy came home with a big zero at the top of his paper.
"Billy, what does this mean?" asked his mother.
"Oh," Billy explained, "my teacher ran out of stars, so she gave me a moon."

The worst thing about naming your baby
is realising how many people you hate.

When your toddlers become teenagers, don't forget to wake
them up at 3am to tell them that your sock came off.

———

Great parenting lies somewhere in the great void between
"Don't do that!" and "Whatever..."

———

My wife and I have decided we don't want children. If anyone wants them, we'll drop them off tomorrow.

———

A teenager agreed to babysit one night for the first time. At bedtime she sent
the children upstairs to bed and settled down to watch TV. Ten minutes later,
a child crept down the stairs, but the girl sent him back to bed. A little later,
the child crept down again and the girl sent him back upstairs again.
This continued for an hour or so. At 9pm the doorbell rang.
It was the next-door neighbour, asking whether her son was there.
The teenager replied, "No."
But just then, a little head appeared over the banister and shouted,
"I'm here, Mum, but she won't let me go home!"

Five-year-old Maisy was in the bath and her mum was washing her hair. She said to Maisy, "Wow, your hair is growing quickly. You need a haircut again!"
Maisy replied, "Maybe you should stop watering it so much."

Welcome to the world of being a parent to a teenager.
Get used to sulking, eye rolling and emotional outbursts.
And as for the teenager...

Freddy was feeling pretty proud of himself.
"Mum, the new puzzle you bought me said three to five years, but I finished it in eighteen months!"

> **YOU KNOW YOUR CHILDREN ARE GROWING UP WHEN THEY STOP ASKING YOU WHERE THEY CAME FROM AND START REFUSING TO TELL YOU WHERE THEY'RE GOING.**

I saw a sign that said, 'Watch for children' and thought, "That sounds like a fair swap."

PARENTING IS...

...constantly informing children how many more minutes
they have of something.

...80% making empty threats and 20% picking up small toys from the floor.

...like a Tarantino film – lots of questions, violence and screaming.

...a journey (except it's just travelling from room to room putting away the same
toys all day long).

...50% love, 10% lies, 10% shouting and 30% unblocking toilets.

...taking longer to get everyone in the car than it takes
to drive to your destination.

...accepting that at least half of all your conversations will be about poo.

...when your 'parent voice' is so loud that even the next-door neighbours
brush their teeth and put on their pyjamas.

...helping your child to search for their chocolate, which you ate
while they were in bed last night.

...being able to open a bar of chocolate or packet
of crisps in complete silence.

My daughter asked me what it's like to be a mum, so I kept on interrupting her every ten seconds until she started to cry.

———

I wish I was as brave as my son.
He just ate three bites of the dinner his mum spent two hours preparing, then asked for a biscuit.

Hell hath no fury like a child whose sibling just pressed the pedestrian crossing button.

Toddlers take half an hour to put on a pair of shoes, but can open three apps, delete iTunes and FaceTime your boss in three minutes.

———

TEACHER: Can you describe yourself in three words?
PUPIL: I. Am. A. Rebel.

Two six-year-olds are chatting to each other in the playground.
One says, "I'm really worried. My dad works 12 hours a day to give me a nice home and good food to eat. My mum spends the whole day cleaning, cooking and running around for me. I'm worried sick!"
The other child says, "What have you got to worry about? It sounds like you've got it made!"
The first kid replies, "But what if they try to escape?!"

HOW MANY TEENAGERS DOES IT TAKE TO CHANGE A LIGHT BULB? ONE. THEY JUST HOLD UP THE BULB AND THE WORLD REVOLVES AROUND THEM.

"No one likes me at school," said Fred to his mother. "The kids don't and the teachers don't. I want to stay at home today."
"You have to go, Son," she insisted. "You're not ill and you have work to do. Besides, you're 45 years old and you're the headmaster."

HOW TO PREPARE FOR NIGHT TIMES WITH A NEW BABY:

Walk around the living room from 5pm to 10pm carrying a wet bag weighing about 5kg, with a radio tuned to static (or some other obnoxious sound) playing loudly.

At 10pm, put the wet bag down, set the alarm for midnight and go to sleep.

Get up at midnight and walk the wet bag around the living room again until 1am.

Set the alarm for 3am.

As you can't get back to sleep, get up at 2am and make a cup of tea.

Go to bed at 2.45am.

Get up again at 3am when the alarm goes off.

Sing songs in the dark until 4am.

Set the alarm for 5am.

Get up when the alarm goes off and make breakfast.

WHY DOES **PSYCHOANALYSIS** WORK FASTER ON MEN THAN WOMEN

and other **GENDER-BASED GIGGLES**

A recent study has found that women who carry a little extra weight
live longer than the men who mention it.

Arguing with my wife is a lot like trying to read the
Terms of Use when connecting to hotel Wi-Fi.
In the end, I just give up and say "I Agree."

What's the difference between a male and female astronaut?

If the crew gets lost in space, the female astronaut
will stop and ask for directions.

OK Google.
How do I disable the autocorrect function on my wife?

FOR ALL THE GUYS WHO THINK A WOMAN'S PLACE IS IN THE KITCHEN,
REMEMBER THAT'S WHERE THE KNIVES ARE KEPT.

A woman hangs up after about half an hour on the phone.
Her husband is surprised and says, "Wow! That was quick. Usually you girls
are at it for at least two hours."
"Yeah, it was a wrong number," his wife replies.

Thomas is 42 years old and single.
Over an evening beer his friend asks him,
"Thomas, why aren't you married?"
Thomas replies, "Well, I've met lots of women
I wanted to marry, but when I bring them home
to meet my parents, my mother doesn't like them."
His friend thinks for a moment and says,
"I've got the perfect solution, why don't you find
a girl who's just like your mother."
A few months later they meet again and his friend
says, "So, did you ever find that perfect girl?"
With a frown on his face, Thomas answers,
"Yes, I found the perfect girl. She was just like
my mother.
You were right, my mother liked her very much."
The friend says, "So what's the problem?"
Thomas replies, "My father hates her."

I told my wife I thought she was drawing her eyebrows too high.

She looked surprised.

Why are dumb-blonde jokes so short?

So men can remember them.

If Laura, Kate and Sarah go out for lunch, they will call each other Laura, Kate and Sarah. If Mike, Dave and John go out, they will affectionately refer to each other as Fat Boy, Godzilla and Peanut.

My wife wants to talk to me about my childish behaviour. There's no way she's getting inside my den without the password.

Wife: I look fat. Can you give me a compliment?

Husband: Your eyesight is perfect.

I just asked my husband if he remembers what today is.

Scaring men is so easy.

Why did God make Adam before Eve?

Because he didn't want anyone telling him how to make Adam.

WHY DOES PSYCHOANALYSIS WORK FASTER ON MEN THAN WOMEN?

BECAUSE WHEN IT'S TIME TO GO BACK TO CHILDHOOD,

MEN ARE ALREADY THERE.

My girlfriend and I often laugh about how competitive we are.

But I laugh more.

A man approached a very beautiful woman in the supermarket and asked, "I've lost my wife in here. Can you talk to me for a couple of minutes?"

"Why?" she asked.

"Because every time I talk to a beautiful woman, my wife appears out of nowhere," he replied.

One morning a wife drew her husband's attention to the couple next door and said, "Do you see them? He tells her every morning how beautiful she is before he leaves for work and gives her a huge kiss. Why don't you do that?"

"I've tried," said the husband, "but she won't let me!"

My husband and I have been married for 63 years.
We've never even thought about divorce.
Murder, yes, but not divorce.

Marriage is an institution of three rings.
An engagement ring, a wedding ring and suffering.

What's the main difference between a woman and a man?
A wo.

My friend just got a puppy. It's incredibly cute and playful and she loves it so much. Unfortunately her husband is allergic to it, so she's going to have to get rid of him.

If you're interested, please send a message.

His name is Michael, he's 54 years old, semi house-trained and weighs 14 stone.

A man is being arrested by a female police officer, who informs him, "Anything you say can and will be held against you." The man replies, "Boobs!"

A desperate woman visits a powerful witch to ask for her help. She asks the witch if she has the ability to break a curse that was cast against her eight years ago.

The witch says, "That depends. What sort of a curse was it?"

To which the woman replies, "It went, 'I now pronounce you man and wife.'"

There are two times in his life when a man doesn't understand a woman.

Before marriage and after marriage.

A beautician says to a client, "Did the face pack I gave you for your girlfriend work?"

The client replies, "It did for a while. Then it fell off."

A husband says to his wife, "Will you love me when I'm fat and bald?"

"Of course I do," she replies.

How does a man show his wife that he is planning for the future?

When he goes to the supermarket, he buys two crates of beer.

I WROTE A PERSONAL AD, SEEKING A HUSBAND. AMAZINGLY, I'VE HAD HUNDREDS OF REPLIES. THEY ALL SAY THE SAME THING — "TAKE MINE."

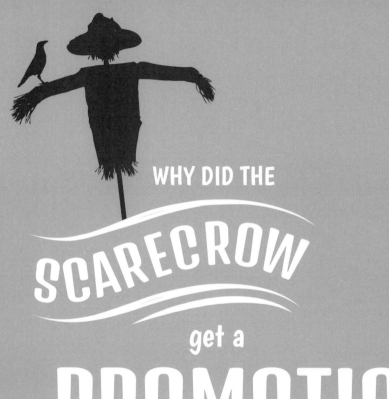

WHY DID THE

SCARECROW

get a

PROMOTION

AND OTHER WORKPLACE WITTICISMS

Nothing ruins a Friday more than realising it's actually only Tuesday.

A man shows up two hours
late for work one day.
His boss yells at him,
"You should've been here at 8.30!"
"Why? What happened at 8.30?"
the man replies.

Two colleagues, a man and a woman, are talking in the office one day.
The woman says, "I can make the boss give me the day off."
The man replies, "And how will you do that?"
The woman says, "Just wait and see."
She then hangs upside down from the ceiling.
The boss comes in and says, "What are you doing?"
The woman replies, "I'm a light bulb."
The boss says, "You've been working so hard that you've gone crazy.
You need to take the day off."
The man starts to follow her and the boss asks, "Where are you going?"
The man says, "I'm going home too. I can't work in the dark."

Why did the can crusher leave his job?

Because it was soda pressing.

———

How is Christmas like your job?

You do all the work and the fat bloke in the suit gets all the credit.

———

Why did the scarecrow get a promotion?

He was outstanding in his field.

A man was walking down the street one day and saw a sign
in a shop window that said 'Help wanted'.
So he ran inside and yelled out, "What's wrong?"

What do your boss and a Slinky have in common?

They're both fun to watch tumble down the stairs.

———

BOSS: Working hard here, Tom?
TOM: Ever since I heard you coming down the stairs, boss!

REASONS TO GO TO WORK NAKED:

Nobody will steal your chair.

It will divert attention away from the fact that you also came to work drunk.

On the morning coffee run you can say,
"I'd love to chip in, but I left my wallet in my trousers."

Your boss will never say,
"I want to see your backside in here by 8am."

My boss told me to have a good day. So I went home.

I just lost my job as a psychic. I did not see that coming.

My boss called me into her office today.

She said, "We both know you're not the brightest spark here, Darren, but over the last five years you've never been sick or late, and I think you deserve a reward. So, how does a brand-new car sound?"

"Vrooom! Vrooooom!" I replied.

71

I got a job answering other people's phones.

It's not for me.

———

Sometimes I just think, to hell with this. I'm going to leave my job
and become a stripper.
Then I remember I'm fat and I can't dance.

———

According to my boss, being 'sick of being here' is not a valid illness
and reason to go home.

———

I asked the HR officer to send me on a yoga course.
He said, "How flexible are you?"
I said, "I can't make Tuesdays."

———

My boss asked, "Do you think you can come in on Saturday this week?
I know you enjoy your weekends, but I really need you here."
I replied, "Yeah, no problem. I'll probably be late though, as the public
transport system is bad at weekends."
He said, "OK, when do you think you'll get here by?"
I said, "Monday."

SIGNS THAT YOU SPEND TOO MUCH TIME AT THE OFFICE:

You get excited when it's Saturday because you can wear jeans to work.

You refer to the tomatoes growing in your garden as 'deliverables'.

You find you really need PowerPoint to explain what you do for a living.

You normally eat out of vending machines.

You know the receptionist better than your next-door neighbour.

You ask your friends to 'think outside the box' when making plans for Friday night.

You think a 'half day' means leaving at 5 o'clock (even if you work at home).

A new employee stood before the paper shredder in his office, looking confused.

"Do you need some help?" a colleague asked.

"Yes," he replied. "How does this thing work?"

"Simple," she said, taking the important report from his hand and feeding it into the shredder.

"Thanks," he said, "but where do the copies come out?"

I ALWAYS GIVE 100% AT WORK.

13% ON MONDAY,
20% ON TUESDAY,
40% ON WEDNESDAY,
21% ON THURSDAY,
AND 6% ON FRIDAY!

One day, a crow was sitting high up in a tree doing nothing.

Along hopped a rabbit who saw the crow, and said to him, "That looks great, can I sit like you and do nothing all day?"

The crow answered, "Sure, why not?"
So the rabbit sat on the ground below the crow and rested.

All of a sudden a fox appeared, jumped on the rabbit and ate it.

Moral: To get away with sitting and doing nothing, you must be sitting very, very high up.

WORK EMAILS YOU WISH YOU'D NEVER SENT:

The email complaining about the colleague who always presses 'reply all', sent as a 'reply all' to the whole company.

The email asking your boss, who shares the same name as your husband, "What's for dinner?"

The email complaining about a colleague, sent to said colleague.

The flirty email outing your own secret office romance, mistakenly sent to the whole company rather than just your partner in crime.

The application for a new job sent to your (now-ex) boss.

The email making fun of a client's ridiculous name, sent to that client.

The email asking if you can sack a specific employee, sent to him instead of your line manager.

The email containing photos from your Christmas do of your workmate passed out, bum in the air, that you meant to send to said workmate for a private laugh, but have just sent to a client sharing the same first name.

WHAT DO YOU CALL A

DOG

MAGICIAN

and other
ANIMAL ANTICS

What do you call a dog magician?

A Labracadabrador.

———

A dog goes into a bar and orders a Martini.
The bartender says, "You don't see a dog in here drinking a Martini very often."
The dog says, "At these prices, I'm not surprised."

———

What do you call a dog that meditates?
Aware wolf.

———

A couple drove down a country road for several miles after an argument,
neither saying a word. As they passed a farm with cows, goats and pigs,
the husband asked sarcastically, "Relatives of yours?"
"Yep," the wife replied. "In-laws."

———

What do you get if you cross a rottweiler and a hyena?

I don't know, but I recommend you join in if it laughs.

What sound do porcupines make
when they kiss?

Ouch!

DOGS ARE TOUGH.
I'VE BEEN INTERROGATING THIS ONE FOR HOURS
AND HE STILL WON'T TELL ME WHO'S A GOOD BOY.

Mummy dog to her pups: We're eating dinner soon.
Don't fill up on homework.

A boy with a monkey on his shoulder was walking down the road
when he passed a police officer, who said, "Now, now, lad, I think you
had better take that monkey to the zoo."

The next day, the boy was walking down the road with the monkey
on his shoulder again, when he passed the same police officer.

The officer said, "Hey there, I thought I told you to take
that monkey to the zoo!"

The boy answered, "I did! Today I'm taking him to the cinema."

A police officer attends the scene of a car crash. As he looks around, the owner's pet monkey pops out of the car. The officer looks down at the monkey and says, "I wish you could tell me what happened here."

The monkey looks up at the officer and nods his head up and down. "Can you understand what I'm saying?" asks the officer. Again, the monkey nods. "Did you see what happened?" asks the officer.

The monkey pretends to have a drink in his hand and turns it up to his mouth. "Were your owners drinking?" asks the officer. The monkey nods his head.

"What else?" he asks. The monkey motions 'kissing'.

"They were kissing too?" asks the officer. The monkey nods his head. "You're saying your owners were drinking and kissing before the crash?"

The monkey nods again. "What were you doing during all this?" 'Driving' motions the monkey.

A man takes his bulldog to the vet and says, "My dog is cross-eyed. Is there anything you can do for him?"

The vet thinks for a few seconds and replies, "Let's have a look at him." The vet picks up the dog while examining his eyes. At long last, he says, "I'm going to have to put him down."

"What? Just because he's cross-eyed?"

"No, because he is really, really heavy."

A blind man walks into a shop with his guide dog. All of a sudden, he raises the dog's lead and begins swinging the dog over his head. The manager runs up to the man and yells, "What are you doing?" The blind man replies, "Just looking around."

A woman was debating with her friend, which was smarter – her cat, or her friend's dog? The first woman said, "My dog is so clever, every morning he waits for the paper boy to come around, and then he takes the newspaper from him and brings it to me."

"I know," the second woman replied.

"How?" said her friend.

"My cat told me," she replied.